Why do crabs walk sideways?

Anna Claybourne

Miles

First published in 2012 by Miles Kelly Publishing Ltd
Harding's Barn, Bardfield End Green, Thaxted,
Essex, CM6 3PX, UK

2 4 6 8 10 9 7 5 3 1

Publishing Director Belinda Gallagher
Creative Director Jo Cowan
Volume Design Redmoor Design, Kayleigh Allen
Cover Designer Kayleigh Allen
Image Manager Liberty Newton
Indexer Jane Parker
Production Manager Elizabeth Collins
Reprographics Stephan Davis, Thom Allaway

ISBN 978-1-84810-616-1

Printed in China

British Library Cataloguing-in-Publication Data

A catalogue record for this book is
available from the British Library

ACKNOWLEDGEMENTS
The publishers would like to thank the following
artist who has contributed to this book:
Mike Foster (character cartoons)
All other artwork from the Miles Kelly Artwork Bank

The publishers would like to thank the following
sources for the use of their photographs:

Fotolia Front cover javarman;
22 Vladimir Ovchinnikov; 28 SLDigi
Shutterstock.com 4 RoxyFer; 5 Photodynamic;
8 Specta; 9 javarman; 16 Glenn Price;
18 Jay Hood; 26 Niar

All other photographs are from:
Corel, digitalSTOCK, digitalvision, John Foxx, PhotoAlto,
PhotoDisc, PhotoEssentials, PhotoPro, Stockbyte

Every effort has been made to acknowledge the
source and copyright holder of each picture.
Miles Kelly Publishing apologises for any
unintentional errors or omissions.

Made with paper from a sustainable forest

Contents

How long is the seashore?

Around the world there are thousands of kilometres of seashore. It can be sandy, pebbly, muddy, or rocky with high cliffs. Many interesting plants and animals make their homes on or near the shore – and so do millions of people.

Sandy seashore

4

Which shores are the coldest?

The coldest seashores are around the North and South poles, the chilliest ends of the Earth. It is so cold here that the sea often freezes. Polar bears, penguins and seals are good at surviving on these icy shores.

Crabeater seal

Find out
Do you live by the sea? If not, look on a map to find your nearest seashore.

Trees in the breeze

Seashores can be blasted by winds from the sea that constantly blow in the same direction. These winds can make trees grow over to one side.

Why do seashores have tides?

Because the Earth is spinning! As Earth spins, the Moon pulls on the sea, and the surface rises. Water flows up the shore, making a high tide. Then it flows out again, creating a low tide. Each seashore has two high tides a day.

Why do seashells cling to rocks?

They cling to rocks so they don't get washed away by the tide. Animals such as limpets, mussels and barnacles live inside seashells. At high tide they open their shells to find food. At low tide, the shells shut tight so they don't dry out.

Limpet

Barnacles

Mussels

write

When you next visit a sandy beach, try writing your name in the sand with a stick.

What are seashore zones?

The area between high and low tide is called the intertidal zone. Low tide zone is wettest, and has lots of seaweed. High tide zone is drier, and has more land plants.

Fun at the beach

Sandy beaches make a great place for sports, such as horseriding, kite-flying, football and volleyball.

How big are the biggest waves?

Winds make waves, which break onto the seashore. Some waves can be 30 metres high – taller than a tower of 18 people. The biggest waves are tsunamis, caused by earthquakes shaking the sea. The tallest ever was 500 metres high!

what is a coral reef?

A coral reef is like a giant seashell. Tiny animals called coral polyps build up layers of hard, colourful coral over many years, to use as a home. It also makes a good home for other sea creatures, such as fish, rays, octopuses, turtles and crabs.

Coral reef

why do crabs walk sideways?

If crabs want to move quickly, walking sideways is best! Their flat, wide bodies help them slip into narrow hiding places. This means that their legs only bend sideways. Crabs can walk forwards, but only very slowly.

sharks in the shallows

Some sharks, like the black-tip reef shark, are often found swimming around coral reefs in search of a snack.

Do all crabs have shells?

Most crabs have a hard shell, but hermit crabs don't. They need to find some kind of 'shell' to protect their soft bodies. Usually, they use another sea creature's old empty shell.

Christmas Island red crab

Make

Make a hermit crab from modelling clay, and give it a home made of a shell, cup or plastic lid.

9

Why do birds love the seaside?

Great black-backed gull

Lesser black-backed gull

Herring gull

Rock dove

Chough

Guillemot

Many kinds of seabird live on and near the seashore. It's a good place to find food and raise their chicks. Seabirds make their nests on the shore or on rocky cliff ledges. They fly out over the water to catch fish.

Razorbill

Puffin

which b...
its wing...
to dry?

The cormorant...
catch fish. Its fe...
soak up the wc...
making it easie...
stay underwate...
hunt. After fishi...
cormorant spre...
wings to dry th...

Tiger beetle

Do beetles head for the beach?

The tiger beetle does! This shiny, green beetle lays its eggs in warm, sandy places. These beetles are often found in sand dunes — small, grassy hills of sand at the top of a beach.

Paint
Copy the picture on this page and paint a tiger beetle. Add green glitter for its shiny body.

Swimming cats
Some tigers live in mangrove forests near the coast. They like to splash in the water to cool down.

HOW fas...
gannet...

Gannets fish by...
then plunging c...
fold their wings...
them, making c...
shape, and car...
water at 100 k...
hour! This lets...
deep into the v...

HOW does being sick help a chick?

Fulmars are seabirds. When they go fishing, they leave their chicks alone in their nests. If hunting animals come near the nests, the chicks squirt stinky, fishy, oily vomit to scare them away!

Does the seashore have shapes?

Sea stacks   Arch

Yes, seashores have lots of shapes. There are bays, spits, cliffs, archways and towers. They form over many years, as wind and waves batter the coast. Softer rocks get carved away into bays and hollows. Harder rocks last longer, and form sticking-out headlands.

Shingle spit

Shingle beach

Bay

Make

At a pebbly beach, make a sculpture by balancing small pebbles on top of each other in a tower.

(partial text from previous page)

impossible
keep the
animals th
eat them.

Thin

Apart from
can you thir
any other an
that lay eg
Use a boo
help y

why are pebbles round?

The pebbles on beaches are stones that have been rolled and tumbled around by waves. As they knock together, they lose their sharp corners and edges, and slowly become smooth and round.

Cave

Cliffs

Delta

what is sand made of?

Sand is made of tiny pieces of rocks and shells. Larger lumps gradually break down into grains, as the waves crash onto them and make them swirl around.

Sandy beach

plastic sand

On some beaches, one in every ten sand grains is actually made of plastic. It comes from litter dropped on beaches or thrown from boats.

why is a curlew's beak so long?

To find its food buried in the mud, a curlew needs a long, thin beak! It sticks its beak deep into the mud to pick out worms, crabs and insects. A curlew also has long legs to wade in the water.

Curlew

measure

With a long ruler, mark out one square metre. Try to imagine thousands of seashells living in this area!

Are seashells different shapes?

Yes, they are. A seashell's shape depends on the creature that lives in it, and how it feeds and moves. Spireshells and tower shells are spirals. Clams and cockles have two hinged shells. They open them to feed, or close them to keep safe.

Clam

Tower shell

Common cockle

Laver spireshell

Painted top shell

How do penguins get out of the water?

Penguins can't fly, but they can swim fast underwater, using their wings as flippers. When they want to get out of the sea, they zoom up to the surface and shoot out of the water, landing on the ice.

crowds of creatures

Some muddy beaches have more then 50,000 tiny shellfish living in each square metre of mud.

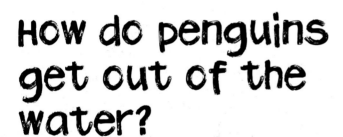

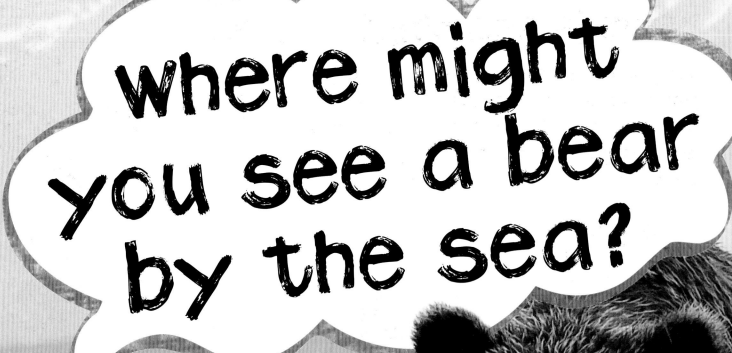

where might you see a bear by the sea?

You might see a bear at an estuary, the place where a river meets the sea. In parts of Canada and the United States, grizzly bears try to catch salmon as they leave the sea and head up rivers to breed. They may also nibble berries and sea plants.

Grizzly bear

what is sea pink?

Sea pink is a seashore flower. Not many plants can survive near the sea because it's so windy and salty. But sea pink is tough. It also has special parts that carry salt out of the plant through its leaves.

Sea pink

Down in one

Penguins swallow fish whole, and the fish dissolve inside their stomachs. They can bring the mush back up to feed their chicks.

why does glass come from the seashore?

make

Make baby penguin food. Mash tinned tuna with a teaspoon of olive oil. Eat it in a sandwich!

Because it's made from sand! Glass is made by heating sand until it melts and turns clear. Long ago, people burnt sea plants such as glasswort to get chemicals for glass-making.

What hides in the sand?

Worms, shrimps, razorshells and some crabs all burrow down into the sand to hide. At high tide they come out and feed. At low tide, being under the sand helps them to stay damp, and avoid being eaten.

Gull

Shrimps

Worms

Hunt

Go on a beach treasure hunt. Look for different shells, different-coloured pebbles and seaweed.

Razorshell

where is the highest tide in the world?

At the Bay of Fundy in Canada, high tide is super-high! The sea level rises to around 17 metres higher than at low tide. At most beaches, the water is just 2 to 3 metres deeper at high tide.

Treasure-hunting

People love beachcombing too. It's fun to look for interesting creatures, pebbles, shells, or bits of glass that have been rubbed smooth by the sea.

Otter

Lizard

Toad

Crab

which animals go beachcombing?

A line of seaweed, driftwood, shells and litter usually collects at the 'strandline' – the level the high tide flows up to. Seabirds, and other animals such as foxes and otters, go 'beachcombing' along the strandline to look for washed-up crabs and fish to eat.

what is a lagoon?

A lagoon is a bit like a shallow lake, but filled with salty seawater. They form when part of the sea is surrounded by a sandbar or a coral reef. Lagoons are warm, shallow and protected from storms – so they make great homes for wildlife.

Lagoon

Make

Build your own sandcastle at the beach or in a sandpit. How tall can you make it?

which fish can walk on land?

Mudskippers are fish, but they can walk on land! They live in the intertidal zone and can breathe in air or water. They skip over the sand or mud, using their front fins like feet.

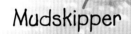

Mudskipper

stingers!

Anemones are seashore creatures with stinging tentacles. They grab and sting prey, then gobble it up!

why do flamingos have long legs?

Flamingos are very tall, pink wading birds. Their long, thin legs help them walk through shallow water in lagoons. They dip their beaks into the water, and use them like a sieve to catch shrimps.

when can you see a rock pool?

When the tide goes out you might see a rock pool. Seawater gets trapped in hollows in rocks or sand. The best places to find rock pools are rocky beaches. Sea creatures shelter here at low tide.

Find out

Find a photo of a sea anemone and a photo of an anemone flower. Do they look alike?

Are there fleas at the beach?

No, there aren't any fleas, but there are little creatures that look like them. Sand hoppers stay buried in the sand all day, then come out at night to look for food.

Sand hopper

What lives in a rock pool?

All kinds of creatures live in a rock pool. These can include crabs, sea anemones, sea urchins, shrimps, shellfish, starfish, sponges, small fish and even octopuses. There are also seaweeds, which animals can hide under.

Rock pool

Super sponges

Rock pool sponges are actually simple animals! The natural sponge that you might use in the bath is a long-dead, dried-out sponge!

which forest grows in the sea?

Mangroves are trees that grow in salty water or seaside mud. Some seashores, especially in hot, tropical places, have mangrove forests growing along them. The mangroves' roots stick out of the ground, and get covered by the tide when it comes in.

Mangroves

Why do crabs turn the ground bright red?

When red crabs march, they turn the ground into a red, moving mass! These crabs live on Christmas Island in the Indian Ocean. Twice a year, thousands of red crabs head to the sea to lay eggs. Then they go back to their forest homes.

PLAY
Have a crab race with your friends. You're only allowed to run sideways, like a crab!

Red crabs

What is a sea cow?

Sea cows aren't really cows. They are dugongs and manatees – huge, sausage-shaped sea creatures, a bit like seals. Like a real cow, sea cows graze on plants, such as sea grass and mangrove leaves.

Fishy cat

In South East Asia there is a wild cat that goes fishing. The fishing cat is a good swimmer, and hunts for fish and other small animals in mangrove swamps.

where do turtles lay their eggs?

Sea turtles live in the sea, but lay their eggs on land. Female turtles crawl up sandy beaches at night, and dig holes with their flippers, in which they lay their eggs. Then they cover them over with sand, and leave them to hatch.

← Turtle

Why do baby turtles race to the sea?

When turtle eggs hatch, baby turtles climb out of their sandy nest and head for the sea. They must reach the water quickly, before they get gobbled up by a seabird, crab or fox.

Salty nose

The marine iguana is a lizard that swims in the sea to eat seaweed. Salt from the sea makes a white patch on its nose.

Find out

There are different types of turtle. Look in books or on the Internet to find out what they are.

Which seabird has a colourful beak?

Puffins have bright beaks striped with orange, yellow and black. In spring, their beaks and feet become brighter, to help them find a mate. Males and females rub their beaks together to show they like each other.

Puffins

Quiz time

Do you remember what you have read about the seashore? Here are some questions to test your memory. The pictures will help you. If you get stuck, read the pages again.

3. Do beetles head for the beach?

page 11

4. Can you tell a pebble from an egg?

page 12

1. How long is the seashore?

page 4

5. Why are pebbles round?

page 15

page 7

2. How big are the biggest waves?

6. Are seashells different shapes?

page 17

7. How do penguins get out of the water?

page 17

11. Are there fleas at the beach?
page 25

page 19

12. What is a sea cow?
page 27

8. Why does glass come from the seashore?

13. Why do baby turtles race to the sea?

page 29

9. What hides in the sand?

page 20

10. Which fish can walk on land?

page 23

Answers

1. Thousands of kilometres long
2. The biggest waves (tsunamis) can be 30 metres high
3. The tiger beetle does
4. You might not be able to, the ringed plover lays eggs that look like pebbles
5. Because they have been rolled and tumbled around by waves
6. Yes they are
7. They zoom up to the surface and shoot out of the water
8. Because it's made from sand
9. Worms, shrimps, razorshells and some crabs
10. The mudskipper
11. No, but there are sandhoppers
12. Dugongs and manatees
13. To avoid being gobbled up by predators

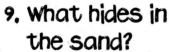

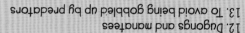

Index